Threads
of
Hope

Threads of Hope

LEARNING TO LIVE WITH DEPRESSION

A COLLECTION OF WRITING EDITED AND
ILLUSTRATED BY FLORA McDONNELL

 SHORT BOOKS

First published in 2003 by
Short Books
15 Highbury Terrace
London N5 1UP

10 9 8 7 6 5 4 3 2 1

A CIP catalogue record for this book
is available from the British Library.

ISBN 1-904095-35-6

Printed in Great Britain by
St. Edmundsbury Press Ltd, Bury St. Edmunds, Suffolk.

Foreword

I have suffered from depression since childhood. But it wasn't until I was 21 that I understood the meaning of the word breakdown. Sheer determination that it wouldn't happen to me again kept me only just afloat until I was 30. Then, the collapse of a brief misguided marriage opened the Pandora's box which I have spent the last seven years trying to come to terms with. On the way I have had four incapacitating breakdowns.

A few years ago, when I was beginning to emerge from my last bout, I was flicking through a glossy magazine. One of the features that caught my eye was a photograph of all sorts of 'it' people wearing T-shirts to promote a campaign for breast cancer awareness.

A cause of this breakdown had been a series of operations

that happened soon after I had come off some antidepressants. A breast lump turned out to be malignant, though luckily self-contained, meaning that beyond the surgery I needed no further treatment. It was a frightening experience, and for a short while I looked my mortality in the face. But at least it was a straightforward fear. My family and my friends were there for me and I could feel their support.

However, three months later, I felt myself sliding towards the irrational terror of everything: a horribly familiar symptom of yet another breakdown. Even though I had the support of a wonderful psychiatrist and therapist, it wasn't any easier. Unable to work, read or even watch television, I was ravaged by anxiety and paralysed by fear. I was able to see everyone I loved, but unable to believe in their support. I couldn't bear to be alone and yet I couldn't bear to be with people. I even doubted my ability to look after my dog who seemed to be afraid of me. The only thing I felt I could do was walk.

I got through it slowly, but so slowly. The world I saw gradually stopped being peopled entirely by bad and sad people. I could hear a robin singing defiantly to the February rain.

*

And so, as I looked at the photograph of all these beautiful successful people advertising breast cancer awareness, I felt a wave of anger rise in my throat. What about depression? Why couldn't they all be wearing T-shirts promoting depression awareness? In my experience, there is no comparison between physical and mental illness. It's never nice to be ill, but at least physical illness doesn't turn your world into a Dali painting.

Out of that moment came the desire to do something. I've been so lucky in many ways. With the bit of extra money I had, I was able to shop around until I found a psychiatrist and a doctor who I really trusted. Never far from the back of my mind is the image of the local psychiatric hospital where, on a stormy night, I had to drop off a man who was lost in mental torment. I just couldn't believe that he would recover in those gulag bunkers.

Poetry, yoga and nature – especially birds – soothed me, but one of the things I have always found comforting, even when I've been at my worst, has been the words of people who have suffered similarly. They could reach me in a way that other people couldn't. Their promises that, in time, it would all dissolve were promises I could remember in the moments when I wasn't totally at sea. I hope that, in the same way, the people who have written here will touch you with their courage and generosity of spirit.

When I was ill, apart from poetry, which became accessible to me for the first time, there were no books I could read – the panoply of self help books was far too daunting. This is the book I was looking for.

Flora McDonnell

June 2002

Most of the writing in this book was written specially for it. But I have also included some poetry and extracts from books I found inspiring. A few of the pieces were written by people who have experienced forms of mental illness other than depression, though I felt that these, too, offered a strong message of hope.

For Dr. Brenda Davies, Dr. Donnette Neil, Helen Gogarty, Eadoin Breathnach, Sarah Matheson, Lola, Dominique, Kieran and Amabel, Peter and Arlene, Raff and Hugh, Rory and Claire, Sian and Peter, Paddy and Catherine, Patrick and Natasha, Henry and Clare, Janet, Hilary, Lanna, Harriet, Lucy B., Lucy I., Potts, Sarah, Kirsty, Xa and Anna, Belinda, Coll, Kate O'S, Kate H., Flora, and my family – especially Alice – who were there for me, and for Thomas.

A percentage of the royalties from this book will be given to various charities

Drop thy still dews of quietness,

Till all our strivings cease;

Take from our souls the strain and stress,

And let our ordered lives confess

The beauty of thy peace.

'Dear Lord and Father of Mankind'
by J.G. Whittier (1807-92)

A Bedtime Story

Once upon a time there was a person
Almost a person

Somehow he could not quite see
Somehow he could not quite hear
He could not quite think
Somehow his body, for instance,
Was intermittent

He could see the bread he cut
He could see the letters of words he read
He could see the wrinkles on handskin he looked at

Or one eye of a person
Or an ear, or a foot, or the other foot
But somehow he could not quite see

Nevertheless the Grand Canyon spread wide open
Like a surgical operation for him
But somehow he had only half a face there
And somehow his legs were missing at the time
And though somebody was talking he could not hear
Though luckily his camera worked O.K.
The sea-bed lifted its privacy
And showed its most hidden fish-thing
He stared he groped to feel
But his hands were funny hooves just at the crucial
                              moment
And though his eyes worked
Half his head was jellyfish, nothing could connect
And the photographs were blurred
A great battleship broke in two with a boom
As if to welcome his glance
An earthquake shook a city onto its people

Just before he got there
With his rubber eye his clockwork ear
And the most beautiful girls
Laid their faces on his pillow staring him out
But somehow his eyes were in the wrong way round
He laughed he whispered but somehow he could not
                                    hear

He gripped and clawed but somehow his fingers
                        would not catch

Somehow he was a tar-baby
Somehow somebody was pouring his brains into a
                        bottle

Somehow he was already too late
And was a pile of pieces under a blanket
And when the seamonster surfaced and stared at the
                        rowboat

Somehow his eyes failed to click
And when he saw the man's head cleft with a hatchet
Somehow staring blank swallowed his entire face
Just at the crucial moment
Then disgorged it again whole

As if nothing had happened

So he just went and ate what he could
And did what he could
And grabbed what he could
And saw what he could

Then sat down to write his autobiography

But somehow his arms were just bits of stick
Somehow his guts were an old watch-chain
Somehow his feet were two old postcards
Somehow his head was a broken windowpane

'I give up,' he said. He gave up.

Creation had failed again.

(Virginia Ironside suggested including this poem for its vivid description of how it feels to be in the darkest depths of depression)

Virginia Ironside

Writer, Agony Aunt

When I'm depressed – which I have been for long periods of my life – I feel as if a grey, leaden liquid has been injected into my brain, slowly leaking down into my body so that every action, however small, feels as if it's executed through thick treacle. The idea of living – or existing, rather, because being depressed doesn't feel like living – fills me with dread.

Advice to 'Go for a walk in the country' or 'Listen to wonderful music' is useless, because the very nature of depression is that it makes me incapable of enjoying anything.

It also prevents me from relating to the outside world.

Twin towers can fall, loved ones can marry and give birth – who cares? Depression removes me from every kind of joy and every kind of disaster. It involves, for me, a shutting off from life. It is the cruellest and loneliest of illnesses.

A kindly, but clueless, friend once said to me: 'You may be depressed, but thank your lucky stars you're not in a concentration camp!' My reaction was that I would far rather be in a concentration camp than be depressed. At least I'd be in it together with other people. At least, even if the prospect of living wasn't likely, we would all *really* want to live.

If you're depressed, my advice would be:

Don't shun medication. It sometimes works miracles and there are lot of different things to try.

Cognitive therapy is the only sort that has been shown to help. Don't go in for anything else unless you're feeling strong and well.

Try to distinguish between yourself and the depression, and realise that all your gloomy thoughts are depression speaking, not you. For instance: 'I am going mad, I'm evil, the world would be better off without me, this depressing view I have of life is actually the true one and everyone else is living in a fantasy world' – these thoughts are symptoms of depression. They're not true.

If you feel suicidal, make a suicide date in your diary for next year. That way you'll stop thinking about it and feel relieved you only have one more year of horror. The chances of your feeling the same in a year are minuscule, but that isn't the point.

When I told a friend I wanted to kill myself, he said: 'Well, why don't you?' It's quite a good question to ask yourself.

Read the Book of Job. It's an enormous comfort to find someone else who understands how you're feeling.

If you're reaching for the bottle, remember that. long-term, alcohol is actually a depressant in itself.

Ring the Samaritans. You don't have to feel suicidal, just low. They can help. And even if they can't, the chat at least kills ten minutes of depression time.

FINALLY, to the people bereaved by suicide: your loved

ones never wanted to kill themselves. They only wanted to kill the pain they were feeling. Unfortunately, there was no other way to achieve this than to throw the baby out with the bath water.

Anonymous

Toy designer

For years I suffered an inner, confusing sadness. To be truly happy or content did not seem possible – this was something which others felt and somehow I did not. The thought process was simple – I was always going to feel sad and this is what I deserved because, aged seven, I had allowed myself to become a victim of child abuse. I had allowed myself to become tainted. I now was dirty, alone and cold. I was too frightened to listen to myself or others, as I knew what it was like to have one's trust betrayed. I accepted inner loneliness and fear, even when surrounded by family and friends, because this felt familiar.

One person changed this for me. When I turned 25,

the sadness became too much to control myself and I sought professional help and, after several dead-ends, I found a therapist who was the first person who saw the sadness.

Being a victim of child abuse did not mean I was a failure to the outside world. I achieved impressively at school, university and in my career. The reality is that I have looked to outside sources to build my confidence as the inside was empty.

As a child, I withdrew from my parents' love as I no longer knew who I could trust. If they hugged me, did this mean that they wanted something more? As a teenager, I was unable to set boundaries – my body was for sale. If you lose your innocence as a child, what is there to hold on to? As I grew older, I was unable to choose suitable, loving partners as friendship plus sex, plus abuse was familiar.

Today, through working with my therapist and with the love of my husband, I have grown to believe that abuse is not OK. I still suffer depression because I carry a deep inner sadness. Deep inside are the tears, fear, pain of a seven-year-old girl, terrified into silence.

But now I am rebuilding myself, asking for love and, most of all, learning to love myself. Today I trust love in my life without fear of abuse. Above all, there are now times of happiness and true contentment. I believe that I am a stronger and happier person than I have ever been, even before the abuse. Through talking about it, I have moved on from the past. Today I can love and am loved – something which I never believed was possible.

SELIMA HILL

Poet, Dorset

I am a poet – although I don't know why. I would like to say I write poems in order to uplift people but unfortunately it isn't always that simple. My poems are often grim and even frightening. I will offer instead a poem by **Anna Kamienska**, the Polish writer:

Those Who Carry

Those who carry pianos
to the tenth floor
wardrobes and coffins
an old man who with a bundle of wood limps
                     beyond the horizon
a woman with a hump of nettles
a madwoman pushing a pram
full of vodka bottles
they will all be lifted
like a gull's feather like a dry leaf
like an eggshell a scrap of newspaper

Blessed are those who carry
for they shall be lifted

Anonymous

London

When things are at their worst which, it has to be said, can be indescribably dreadful, sometimes the simplest things are all that are bearable. For me, making a cup of tea and trying to entirely concentrate on that, and then drinking it slowly, can help a fraction.

Anonymous

Self-employed, London

My first experience of depression came suddenly. I was sitting in a university library trying to study a book when I found myself thinking suicidal thoughts. About a year afterwards, I was prescribed antidepressants by a doctor, whom I had visited about a stomach problem. His diagnosis and the pills helped me for a while, but 18 months later I was still in a bad way. I felt I had to withdraw from the world and rebuild myself.

I was very lucky because I found someone who was able to help me. I was his patient for six years. My family and friends supported me too, but it was the carefully constructed world of his consulting room that helped me the

most. He had no agenda for me, except that I should find out what I really wanted for myself. That was a revelation, as I had always felt that people were judging me and expecting things of me. I was a frightened child in an adult's body. My journey to autonomous adulthood was severely disrupted, but it has been resumed.

Singing is my therapy now. I am finding my voice. As a child, I was told that I couldn't sing. I didn't live comfortably in my body; my feet were not on the ground and my strength was blocked. I was brought up to use my head, but not my body or my feelings. Reason and conscious thought were the touchstones. Now I have found that I have more strength than I ever dreamed of. Singing helps me to trust myself and to follow my instincts. I have always been a 'control freak', but now I am learning that the less I try to control, the stronger I am. Approval, security and control. If, a little at a time, we relax the struggle to find those three things, life becomes much easier.

'ANASTASIA'

North-west England

And they threw away the key

Another morning waking up in the Wing – no bird-song here but the sounds and the smells of my tormented neighbours. I look bewilderedly around me – a mattress on the floor, a degrading canvas gown and a pot to piss in. And that was it. Period.

The Wing was for people who 'They' had given up on. There were five of us locked in cells which were a prison within a prison – this was officially a hospital for the criminally insane. I hadn't had a conversation or left the cell for months – summer had passed me by.

Every day, every day, the routine of isolation and craziness went on – except that today was different. Today was Christmas Day – wasn't it?

I heard the rattling of keys and knew that breakfast was on its way. It had to be bacon and eggs – Christmas Day was the only day we had bacon and eggs for breakfast. All greasy and congealed because they were cooked overnight.

Aah, I was right, here it was. 'They' opened the door – there were always at least two of them – one to watch the other's back.

I raised a question.

'When Father Donnelly comes to see the other Catholic girls – can I go to pray with them?'

Answer: 'Father Donnelly won't be coming today – it's Tuesday.'

Me: 'It's Christmas Day. Father is sure to come.'

Them: 'No, it isn't Christmas Day – that was yesterday.'

They were laughing at me.

I'd missed Christmas.

I picked up the plate of greasy breakfast and threw it at them. It missed them and landed in a greasy lump.

Damn. No breakfast this morning.

I sat on my mattress on the floor, hopeless and helpless – hopeless because of my illness and helpless against the cruelty of the 'nurses'.

I used to pass the hours by trying to remember the plot of books I had read – the 'goodies' and the 'baddies' and all their names and actions. I wasn't allowed to have books. How do they expect you to get well if the only companion you have is your own madness?

I had lost track of time until suddenly the cell door was opened by a German nurse called Wally. And she had brought with her – who? Yes, it was Father Donnelly.

He came into my room carrying a small wooden chair, and put two lighted candles on the chair, making a little altar in this Dungeon of Despair.

I knelt down with him and we prayed together and he gave me Holy Communion. And as we prayed, I felt all the months of confusion and illness just drain through me, to be replaced by a kind of peace and calmness. I can't remember or explain how it happened, only that by the time Father Donnelly had give me his Blessing I really did feel blessed and peaceful.

So, on that Christmas morning after months of isolation, I was allowed to get dressed and go into the Day Room for a few hours. I had Christmas lunch with the other patients on the ward. I think perhaps that year I found out what Christmas was all about.

Lord Stevenson of Coddenham, CBE

Chairman of HBOS plc and Pearson plc, London

Some ten years ago I left London to spend August in our cottage in Suffolk. God was in his heaven and all was well with the world. I was financially secure even buoyant; in worldly terms I was much admired and seemed to be successful; furthermore, I had a hugely satisfying private life with my wife, children and friends. I can remember going into Gap and buying some clothes for the summer with a definite sense of smugness.

Forty-eight hours later I was in the grip of persistent anxiety which turned into clinical depression. There was no rhyme or reason for it that I or medical science could understand; it is difficult to describe the sense of hopelessness – the 19th-century concept of 'melancholia' perhaps best describes the feeling.

With the help of my wife, I took advice. The advice was that a mixture of drugs and/or cognitive therapy stood a 90 per cent chance of making the world seem attractive again. I did not really believe it at the time, and must have been hell to live with, but I followed my wife's advice of taking one day at a time.

Over a six-to-nine-month period the advice proved correct. It is worth observing that I combined this with continuing to lead a work life that most people would regard as demanding and responsible.

Until this experience, in my heart of hearts I thought that depression was self-imposed and indeed something to be 'snapped out of'. Although I am sure that in 100 years time science will have pinpointed the reason why I inexplicably became ill, there were no obvious reasons for my depression.

Like everyone, I am often down-hearted and 'depressed' because things go wrong. Nothing had gone wrong on this occasion. I had to accept that this was an illness analogous to a viral infection, breaking a leg or whatever. I have since discovered that it is a very common illness suffered at one time or another by a great many people.

SUE CUTTS

Newark, Notts

Life

Pink, blue, white, long, round, big and small. They are in bottles or packets. But in my hand they're harmless. My mind goes round. Shall I, or not? Only I can know.

Still I sit and think. My mind wanders. Chores to do: the washing-up, the hoovering, the dusting. They have to be done.

I look back at my life. If I had given him up at birth, and gone back to work, what would I be doing now? Would my health be the same, or would I be better?

The phone rings. 'Hello, mum.' My son remembers me.

THE DUKE OF RICHMOND AND GORDON

West Sussex

I think that the most reassuring statement made to me during my three-year depression was spoken by my psychiatrist. I asked him in some desperation how much longer it would be before I felt much better and he said, 'I can't tell you how soon, but you will get better,' and I was much better within six months.

I know that there are some who don't get better, but there are many more who do.

JULIAN RENA

Sculptor, London

A friendship I have had for many years has helped me enormously. We have seen each other go through some tough times. She has known me both at my dottiest and most depressed. I can feel and be weak, cowardly, monosyllabic or brainless and she accepts it. She has made me feel it's OK to be like this, and better, she has even helped me to find a kind of light-heartedness.

MARGARET DRABBLE

Novelist, London

I have a number of quotations that come back to me in times of depression and low spirits, and many of them are from **Wordsworth**, the poet whose work rescued John Stuart Mill from his mental breakdown. And of these quotations, perhaps the most inspiring is this, from 'The Prelude':

> **Our destiny, our nature and our home**
> **Is with infinity, and only there;**
> **With hope it is, hope that can never die,**
> **Effort, and expectation, and desire,**
> **And something evermore about to be.**

I love these lines, because they remind us that it is our nature to aspire and suffer and struggle, and that though we may never see happiness ourselves, our very struggle is part of the nature of being human. I find this much more cheering and invigorating than words of false comfort. Wordsworth was a poet who suffered intensely, and rejoiced greatly, and knew that life was a serious matter. In a world awash with triviality, he is greatly to be valued.

ANDREW SOLOMON

Journalist and previous Pulitzer Prize finalist,
and author of many books, including
the novel *A Stone Boat*.

Depression is the flaw in love. To be creatures who love, we must be creatures who can despair at what we lose, and depression is the mechanism of that despair. When it comes, it degrades one's self and ultimately eclipses the capacity to give or receive affection. It is the aloneness within us made manifest, and it destroys not only connection to others but also the ability to be peacefully alone with oneself. Love, though it is no prophylatic against depression, is what cushions the mind and protects it from itself. Medications and psychotherapy can renew that protection, making it easier to love and be loved, and that is why they work. In good spirits, some love themselves and some love others and some love work and some love God: any of these passions can furnish that vital sense of purpose that is the opposite of depression. Love forsakes us from time to time, and we forsake love. In depression, the meaninglessness of every enterprise and every emotion, the meaninglessness of life itself, becomes self-evident. The only feeling left in this loveless state is insignificance.

It can be hard to sustain a sense of humour during an experience that is really not so funny. It is urgently necessary to do so. The most important thing to remember during a depression is this: you do not get the time back. It is not tacked on at the end of your life to make up for the disaster years. Whatever time is eaten by a depression is gone forever. The minutes that are ticking by as you experience the illness are minutes you will not know again. No matter how bad you feel, you have to do everything you can to keep living, even if all you can do for the moment is to breathe. Wait it out, and occupy the time of waiting as fully as you possibly can. That's my big piece of advice to depressed people. Hold on to time; don't wish your life away. Even the minutes when you feel you are going to explode are minutes of your life and you will never get those minutes again.

The opposite of depression is not happiness but vitality, and my life, as I write this, is vital, even when sad. I may wake up sometime next year without my mind again; it is not likely to stick around all the time for the rest of my life. Meanwhile, however, I have discovered what I would have to call a soul, a part of myself I could never have imagined until one day seven years ago, when hell came to pay me a surprise visit. It's a precious discovery. Almost every day I feel momentary flashes of hopelessness, and wonder every time whether I am slipping. For a petrifying instant here and there, a lightning-quick flash, I want a car to run me over and I have to grit my teeth to stay on the sidewalk until the light turns green; or I imagine how easily I might cut my wrists; or I taste hungrily the metal tip of a gun in my mouth; or I picture going to sleep and never waking up again. I hate those feelings, but I know that they have driven me to look deeper at life, to find and cling to the reasons for living. I cannot find it in me to regret entirely the course my life has taken. Every day, I choose, sometimes gamely and sometimes against the moment's reason, to be alive. Is that not a rare joy?

AMANDA BROOKE

Housewife, mother of four, Northern Ireland

My depression crept up on me. I'd been low for some time but I think pregnancy and all it brings just tipped me over the edge. I can't remember an exact time, but I do remember a day some years later when I woke up and the black cloud seemed to have lifted slightly. It was remarkable to realise how bad I'd been feeling for so long. When I look back and realise how dark those years were, I wish someone had noticed and helped me. I became so used to the way I felt, I forgot what it was like to feel good. To the outside world I seemed a bit detached, but perfectly all right. I could even laugh occasionally, though it meant nothing.

I'm not sure what changed me – I think it was probably another crisis that I couldn't avoid becoming involved in. Whatever it was, I know that I live on a tightrope. If things begin to go wrong – the weather, insecurity, loneliness – it very soon spirals down again. I'm more aware of the first signs and will try and distract myself. Keeping really busy sometimes helps, but I know it's lurking around the corner.

It doesn't matter how often people tell me how lucky I am – lovely husband, beautiful healthy children, nice house. It just makes me feel guilty and worse. And why do people always ask me 'What's wrong?' and not understand that, if I knew, I wouldn't be feeling like this, would I?

The main thing that stops me putting my head in the oven is my babies. No matter how miserable I feel, I can't stop loving them. I couldn't bear to think of someone else bringing them up or the thought of missing out on a second of their fascinating lives.

*

Things that make me smile and feel the world isn't such a bad place and maybe there is a point to it all:-

My children

Beautiful, uplifting dramatic weather

Making something

Bonfires

Swimming in cold effervescent surf

Fish markets

THE SEA

JOHN COLERIDGE

Retired teacher, writer, East Anglia

'It happens'

It's not easy to be sure, but I think it all began at least a year before. I'd used up every shred of mental energy I had, all my reserves. I was as flat as a thorn-torn inner tube.

This is how it happens, you see.

One morning, I froze. Getting out of bed was impossible. My wife phoned the Head first, and then our GP. Second Master of the school, though I was, I'd run into the infamous Marathon Wall.

'Jean, he's burnt out. Just let him be. No visitors, none.' In answer to her anxious question, he added, 'No pills either.' Though I couldn't for the life of me remember who the man was, I reached out and clawed his shoulder. 'It's all right old fellow. I understand.' 'Thanks,' I think I nodded. He smiled. What he said to Jean in the kitchen, I don't know... but it doesn't matter.

So, day in, day out, I sat watching the Embassy World Snooker, silent, lifeless, almost motionless, eating very little. The Head and his wife came one day – kind folk. 'What are you doing here? PLEASE go.'

It can't have been much fun for Jean. However, shopping had to be done. She didn't use the car; presumably so that I wouldn't know when she was away. I listened. Silence. No radio even in the kitchen. I slipped out back, started up the car and was away. Choosing obscure back lanes where I wouldn't be recognised, I drove for fully an hour. And ran out of petrol. Panic. Exploring fearfully a farmyard track I'd never seen before, I found an old labourer, mucking out a byre. Did he think I was a deaf mute? I led him back to the car and gave him our telephone number. He got through. Jean came, pale and relieved. He refused anything for helping.

Friends come from anywhere.

One day, I spoke. 'Let's go out, darling.' We went to the nearby Country Park. Familiar territory but ... I was cringing, stock-still in the centre of a track. 'What's up, Jim?'

'The trees. They're leaning in. They're smothering me.'

'About turn.' Jean led me home.

Day by day, things improved. I went out on my own, only avoiding people who might recognise me.

We took a cruiser on the Broads. Eventually we slept close at night. IT was over.

Hope happens that way.

DESMOND FITZGERALD, KNIGHT OF GLIN

Writer, art historian and consultant for Christie's, Ireland

The apprehension in the pit of the stomach, the growl of the black dog, pattered relatively late and rather stealthily, into my life in my mid-thirties. The first time it balefully looked round the corner at me was during a holiday in Majorca, when suddenly after the first two idyllic days the rain came down continually for a week and we couldn't get off the island.

A few years later, when my work in London was dividing my loyalties with coming back to look after Glin with my wife and family, the total crunch came, and I remember going to a mind-doctor in Harley Street and, arriving early and looking out of the window, seeing him spring out of his little sports car with a merry laugh, and after one meeting I knew that he was the very last person I wanted to be looked after by.

It was only by chance when staying, speechless, in Canada with my mother in her Arcadian British Columbian garden that I met an English doctor who told me about lithium. My mother refused under any circumstances to accept that I was suffering from depression – 'mononucleosis' (glandular fever) was how she described my symptoms away to her conventional friends.

Lithium has been my saviour ever since, and despite various ebbings and flowings, I have more or less been able to get on with my life without too many black holes of despair and horror.

I write these lines because I have always wanted to tell others that one does get better, life does return to one's tormented and fragile self. It seems to me so vital that people in all walks of life should encourage sufferers not be ashamed, and not to be closet depressives.

I have always wanted to tell the world that hope does

spring afresh from the morass of self-pitying misery into which we plunge. It is far better to face down and dose the growling black dog than lock him up in his kennel and pretend that his anguish doesn't exist.

SIDNEY SMITH, 1771-1845

Clergyman, writer and wit

D^{ear} Lady Georgiana,

...Nobody has suffered more from low spirits than I have done – so I feel for you. 1st. Live as well as you dare. 2nd. Go into the shower-bath with a small quantity of water at a temperature low enough to give you a slight sensation of cold, 75 (degrees) or 80 (degrees). 3rd. Amusing books. 4th. Short views of human life – not further than dinner or tea. 5th. Be as busy as you can. 6th. See as much as you can of those friends who respect and like you. 7th. And of those acquaintances who amuse you. 8th. Make no secret of low spirits to your friends, but talk of them freely – they are always worse for dignified concealment. 9th. Attend to the effects tea and coffee produce upon you. 10th. Compare your lot with that of other people. 11th. Don't expect too much from human life – a sorry business at the best. 12th. Avoid poetry, dramatic representations (except comedy), music, serious novels, melancholy sentimental people, and everything likely to excite feeling or emotion not ending in active benevolence. 13th. Do good, and endeavour to please everybody of every degree. 14th. Be as much as you can in the open air without fatigue. 15th. Make the room where you commonly sit, gay and pleasant. 16th. Struggle by little and little against idleness. 17th. Don't be too severe upon yourself, or underrate yourself, but do yourself justice. 18th. Keep good blazing fires. 19th. Be firm and constant in the exercise of rational religion. 20th. Believe me, dear Lady Georgiana,

Very truly yours,
Sidney Smith

ALICE OSWALD

Poet

Woman in a Mustard Field

From love to light my element
was altered when I fled
out of your house to meet the space
that blows about my head.

The sun was rude and sensible,
the rivers ran for hours
and whoops I found a mustard field
exploding into flowers;

and I slowly came to sense again
the thousand forms that move
all summer through a living world
that grows without your love.

ALASTAIR CAMPBELL

The Prime Minister's Director of Communications
and Strategy, London

When I became Tony Blair's press secretary seven years ago, I knew that the 'skeletons' would probably come out, so I never hid the fact I'd had a nervous breakdown. I'd always been very open about it, calling it my 'mad period'. There's no point pretending I wasn't mad, because I was, probably for some time up to my breakdown, and then it took quite a while to recover. I think people are disarmed when you're up front about it. I've never had anybody say a bad thing about my breakdown.

It happened in 1986 when I was 29. I'd been a journalist at the *Mirror* and was poached by Eddy Shah's *Today* when it was launched. It was a disaster. I'd left a professional and political base I felt totally at home with and gone somewhere I felt a bit alien. I was over-promoted; I hit the bottle pretty hard, got completely manic and cracked.

It's hard to describe coming out of a breakdown. There's a permanent dull ache and occasional stabs of real pain or fear. I can't help smiling when I hear people say they're depressed when what they mean is they're a bit fed up. I do it myself sometimes. But there are not many things as deadening as real depression, when you feel unable to move a muscle and you're incapable of getting out of bed, or speaking or thinking, or doing anything, and you can't see a way forward.

Fiona, my partner, was incredibly supportive, even though it had been a nightmare for her having seen this thing coming and feeling powerless to do anything about it. I slowly rebuilt myself with help from family and friends. It also sorted out who my real friends were and what really mattered to me, and the next year we had our first child which was brilliant. Of course the breakdown was humiliating on one level – journalism is a very gossipy world and people's basic take was that this whiz kid had flown too high, fallen flat on his face and ended up in a 'lunatic asylum'. And I know I was lucky in many ways, and if I hadn't had the support I had it could have ended far, far worse.

But now I look back on it with a real sense of achievement. It was a 24-carat crack-up and I'm proud of the fact I rebuilt myself, did OK as a journalist again and went on to do what I do now. I couldn't have done what I've done in this job without believing what I believe very strongly, and being tough-minded, focused, mentally and physically fit. I feel the breakdown, and the recovery, played a big part in all that. I was taken to the limit, really close to losing everything, at absolute breaking-point, and I think over time that turned me into a stronger person. It was in many ways the worst thing that ever happened to me, certainly the scariest, but in other ways the making of me. I'm very conscious of the fact that for many other people a mental breakdown has anything but that effect, that the suffering never stops, so I've been lucky. One of the reasons I've wanted to be open about it is that I know from my own recovery that it is possible to take strength and hope from the experience of others who've gone to what feels like hell and back and lived to tell the tale.

CATHY McDONNELL

Cook

When I was a newly married young woman, I was plagued with worries and insecurity. I took an overdose. The one thing I remember making a difference then was hearing the doctor say to my husband, 'What a waste.' It really shocked me. I threw myself into being the good wife and mother I felt I should be.

But I suppose really the one thing that has always given me comfort is cooking. When I was a child, my mother allowed and encouraged me to enjoy the kitchen, and I did. In stirring, kneading, rolling, basting, tasting, licking, making something delicious, a treat for me and the people I love, I find real fulfilment; my worries dissolve.

Otherwise, living alone, my dogs are a great comfort. Walking them every day has opened up a new awareness of nature and the seasons, even living in a city.

Sitting in a church of whatever faith is very calming and comforting, especially when there is beautiful choral music.

JOHN MONTAGUE

Poet, short story writer, Ireland

I grew up in pre-Freudian days when there was little or no help available, so I am sympathetic to your cause. This is by way of a mental yoga exercise to clear the head after a hangover, or an overdose, or a prolonged gloom. And it is meant to be swallowed mentally, with the help of humour, like a clear glass of water!

There are Days

There are days when
one should be able
to pluck off one's head
like a dented or worn
helmet, straight from
the nape and collarbone
(those crackling branches!)

and place it firmly down
in the bed of a flowing stream.
Clear, clean, chill currents
coursing and spuming through
the sour and stale compartments
of the brain, dimmed eardrums,
bleared eyesockets, filmed tongue.

And then set it back again
on the base of the shoulders:
well tamped down, of course,
the laved skin and mouth,
the marble of the eyes
rinsed and ready
for love; for prophecy?

ANONYMOUS

Sub-editor, East London

From under the glass

When despair came to keep house in me, hope quietly moved out. I never even noticed that I'd lost hope until one day I heard someone use the word several times and couldn't think what he meant. Puzzled, I went back to contemplating the steepnesses that filled my mind – the riveting, vast fears that had spun my living to glass. That held me fast and out of reach.

After some time, despair nearly rubbed me out altogether. With the last feeble rags of revolution in me, I struggled to communicate.

I'd been so private for so long, people could barely make me out. But I was lucky. One friend did hear that under the words something was wrong. 'You need help,' she said, certainly. 'Proper help.' And she gave me the name and telephone number of a psychotherapist she had heard about.

One early September morning afterwards, I walked through an unfamiliar part of the city to a preliminary interview. As I went, the feeble rags of revolution that had brought me, grew up into flags and began waving the other way.

'*Look!*' they flapped. '*At this rich district. Clearly this "Therapist" will be a quack and a parasite. There will be nothing authentic or compassionate about her. And* you –' they said, '*it is disgusting that you should seek help when everyone else in the world has to help themselves.*'

Inside the house, they positively billowed with scorn. '*See?*' they triumphed, '*Her room is ugly, her manner cold. There is a sofa where clearly you and not she will sit. What a cliché...*'

'Please sit down,' the therapist said. Her smile was

warm and ingenuous and brought her face to life. 'Now tell me why you've come.'

My limbs acted a helpless mime on the sofa, cramping into knots of embarrassment.

She looked at me encouragingly. I made a huge effort and a sentence tore through, followed by tears.

'Go on,' she said gently.

What the hell, I thought, revolution dying in me, sorrow welling. A paragraph surfaced.

After it she did not speak straightaway.

I waited.

Nothing.

They were seconds probably, but to me they were hours.

Paranoid, I flooded the silence with bitter fluency. I took out some steepnesses to frighten her with, making them swing and teeter in the room. Then I busied myself with proving to her that from behind glass, my refracted sight was especially lucid.

Next I said I would go.

'You see,' I told her, 'I'm wasting your time. I needn't be here at all.'

She looked at me, startled. 'But we haven't even begun yet, have we?' she said. 'I'm sorry if I seemed absent a minute ago. I was thinking. You mentioned a brother. Will you tell me more about him?'

My brother...

I stopped trying to go and started to think about him. He was a hurt, lonely man and with all my heart I wished him happy. I described to her the awkward way he walked. My shoulders hunched like his, I explained some jagged things I thought had left their tread in him. I stopped, remembering.

In the quiet, I heard her sigh.

'Is anything wrong?' I asked nervously.

'Not with me,' she said. 'But I am sorry. It is very sad.'

Could it be true? Was there room just for pity? In this big house, this wealthy district, this – therapy?

I relaxed, and slid down several inches of steepness.

Then went on to try to tell her other things – groping to

be natural, hearing against her responses how bent and crooked I had grown.

Finally, I looked at the clock. I had been communicative for almost 40 minutes and felt as thirsty as a camel.

'Shall I go now?' I asked.

She laughed. Just laughed. And I found that I believed in it.

Then she said, 'I think we should start next week.'

At which the flags blew back. '*This is it*,' they warned. '*If you go with this, you admit to being ill, you agree to being a patient, you sign up to having a doctor... You surrender both your independence and your steepnesses. You may even become* well.'

Well. My eyes flicked wildly round the room.

And met her steady gaze.

'Okay,' I said. A little sulkily for the flags' sake.

We made the arrangements for times. Then I set off up the hill to find a tea shop.

As I walked, I saw that the morning was soft, pearl grey, that the plane trees growing on the other side of the street were very tall, and that the faces of the people waiting at the bus stop were each different from the other.

For a few steps there was just enough quiet in me to see out. Just enough rest to find things as they were. I didn't notice this time either, but a little hope had crept back in under the glass.

Anonymous

Artist, South London

My commonsense advice is age-old and is to walk oneself weary.

CHARLOTTE RAVEN

Journalist

For all its pain and strangeness, there is something undeniably wonderful about having your life's purpose defined by your need to recover from addiction or depressive illness.

When I originally went into recovery, all I could do was ask how much longer it would be before I could go back to the things I missed. At that point, I still thought that my depression was caused by a 'chemical imbalance' that could be put right in a jiffy.

It took me months of gently probing therapy sessions and self-interrogation before I realised that the persona I'd adopted with which to protect myself, which I had always thought rather impressive, had not only cost me my sanity, but also pissed off the people I most wanted to attract.

Once you begin to realise all this, it no longer seems quite such a trial to spend much of your week at 12-step meetings and group-therapy sessions. It's an odd truth that, once you've stopped worrying how long it's going to take, the lights go on in the space you're inhabiting and you start to see colour and texture.

Everyone who's been in recovery will understand the power of this moment of total surrender. It's the point in your journey where you stop seeing the thing as a narrative. Instead of wondering how much progress you are making, you realise that this is it. For me, that indifference to outcome could happen only once I'd dropped any idea of the person I dreamt of becoming and stopped checking my reflection for any hint of this transformation. The curious alchemy of recovery can work only when you're not watching out for it. If you check on it every five minutes, it will curdle unpleasantly; if you don't, it will reward you with days that unaccountably seem to fold in all the right places.

MELITA DENARO

Artist, Donegal

I came across this while drawing my mother in a nursing home not long before she died. I had been recently diagnosed with MS. It was a particularly hard time then. And this beautiful poem by **Thomas Hardy** gave me hope because it encourages belief that all will be well.

The Darkling Thrush

I leant upon a coppice gate
    When Frost was spectre-gray,
And Winter's dregs made desolate
    The weakening eye of day.
The tangled bine-stems scored the sky
    Like strings of broken lyres,
And all mankind that haunted nigh
    Had sought their household fires.

The land's sharp features seemed to be
    The Century's corpse outleant.
His crypt the cloudy canopy,
    The wind his death-lament.
The ancient pulse of germ and birth
    Was shrunken hard and dry,
And every spirit upon earth
    Seemed fervourless as I.

(cont.)

At once a voice arose among
　　The bleak twigs overhead
In a full-hearted evensong
　　Of joy illimited;
An aged thrush, frail, gaunt, and small,
　　In blast-beruffled plume,
Had chosen thus to fling his soul
　　Upon the growing gloom.

So little cause for carolings
　　Of such ecstatic sound
Was written on terrestrial things
　　Afar or nigh around,
That I could think there trembled through
　　His happy good-night air
Some blessed Hope, whereof he knew
　　And I was unaware.

Charles Spencer

Theatre critic of the *Daily Telegraph* and novelist, Surrey

A few tips I've found helpful after suffering intermittently from depression over the last 20 years.

If you can get out of bed, do get out of bed.

And if you can face going outside, try and take a brisk walk. It helps more than you think it will.

Try not to dwell on the past or on the future too much. The prospect of an endless dark tunnel ahead is unendurable.

Try to live in the day, doing what you can, but not beating yourself up about it if you manage very little, or nothing at all. Every small task achieved during depression is a triumph of the human spirit.

Don't make the mistake I did and use alcohol as a form of self-medication. The relief is very temporary, the long-term consequences appallingly malign. Booze and prescribed antidepressants really don't mix.

Try prayer, to an unknown higher power, or God as you do or do not understand him:

God grant me the serenity to accept the things I cannot change;
The courage to change the things I can;
And the wisdom to know the difference.

HILARY ALEXANDER

Social worker, Co. Antrim, N. Ireland

I am a social worker and have worked with people who suffer from a range of mental health problems for the last 12 years. Until I was 40, I believed that I understood the meaning of depression – the sadness, the apathy and the boredom that is associated with the illness. Then I experienced it for myself – the insomnia, the paranoia and the terror.

When my GP prescribed Seroxat I was horrified by the idea of the side effects, especially the possibility of putting on weight and that awful feeling of fatigue. (A little knowledge can be a bad thing!) Then I remembered the advice that I had often given to others: 'Don't forget to help yourself; don't just rely on medication to get you better.'

I identified a friend, someone I could confide in who listened and empathised with my fears and sense of inadequacy, which helped me to come to terms with being myself. Their help and support encouraged me to find my feet again, although I recognise that I was fortunate in not having to rely on medication, as I know many people don't have any choice.

Kay Redfield Jamison

Professor of Psychiatry at the Johns Hopkins University
School of Medicine, Baltimore

So why would I want anything to do with this illness? Because I honestly believe that as a result of it I have felt more things, more deeply; had more experiences, more intensely; loved more and been more loved; laughed more often for having cried more often; appreciated more the springs, for all the winters; worn death 'as close as dungarees', appreciated it – and life – more; seen the finest and the most terrible in people, and slowly learned the values of caring, loyalty, and seeing things through. I have seen the breadth and depth and width of my mind and heart and seen how frail they both are, and know how ultimately unknowable they both are. Depressed, I have crawled on my hands and knees in order to get across a room and have done it month after month. But, normal or manic, I have run faster, thought faster, and loved faster than most I know. And I think much of this is related to my illness – the intensity it gives to things and the perspective it forces on me. I think it has made me test the limits of my mind (which, while wanting, is holding) and the limits of my upbringing, family, education, and friends.

*

...We all build internal sea walls to keep at bay the sadnesses of life and the often overwhelming forces within our minds. In whatever way we do this – through love, work, family, faith, friends, denial, alcohol, drugs, or medication – we build these walls, stone by stone, over a lifetime. One of the most difficult problems is to construct these barriers of such a height and strength that one has a true harbour, a sanctuary away from crippling turmoil and pain, but yet low enough, and permeable enough, to let in fresh seawater that will fend off the inevitable inclination toward brackishness. For someone with my cast of mind and mood, medication is an integral element of this wall: without it, I would be constantly beholden to the crushing movements of a mental sea; I would, unquestionably, be dead or insane.

But love is, to me, the ultimately more extraordinary part of the breakwater wall: it helps to shut out the terror and awfulness, while, at the same time, allowing in life and beauty and vitality. After each seeming death within my mind or heart, love has returned to recreate hope and to restore life. It has, at its best, made the inherent sadness of life bearable, and its beauty manifest. It has, inexplicably and savingly, provided not only cloak but lantern for the darker seasons and grimmer weather.

SHEILA BRIGGS-GUDGIN

State-registered nurse and midwife, Nottinghamshire

I have suffered from manic depression most of my adult life. I have had many episodes of depression and made several suicide attempts.

The worst time in my life was when I discovered my husband dead, having hung himself whilst resident in the hostel of the local hospital where I was a patient on the psychiatric ward.

I was devastated. For once in my life I was alone because I had become so dependent on my husband. The only family I had was a half-sister in Australia and an elderly mother. I only had one friend.

Then another patient on the ward who was a Christian

read me the 'Footprints' story. It seemed so relevant to me, and from that moment on my life began to turn around. I even bought a pendant with the last few words engraved on it to remind me of God's love.

Footprints

One night a man had a dream. He dreamed he was walking along the beach with the Lord. Across the sky flashed scenes from his life. For each scene he noticed two sets of footprints in the sand, one belonged to him, and the other to the Lord.

When the last scene of his life flashed before him, he looked back at the footprints in the sand. He noticed that many times along the path of his life there was only one set of footprints. He also noticed that it happened at the very lowest and saddest times in his life.

This really bothered him and he questioned the Lord about it. 'Lord, you said that once I decided to follow you, you'd walk with me all the way. But I have noticed that during the most troublesome times in my life there is only one set of footprints. I don't understand why, when I needed you most, you would leave me.'

The Lord replied 'My precious, precious child, I love you and would never leave you. During your times of trial and suffering, when you see only one set of footprints, it was then that I carried you.'

WENDY COPE

Self-employed writer, Winchester

This poem was written in the first year or two of my psychoanalysis when I was in my late twenties. I had been diagnosed as suffering from 'fairly severe chronic depression' and I was beginning to recover.

The Journey

The journey was difficult at first
Until I shipped my oars,
Let the river sweep me on,
Lifted my eyes from the dark brown water
And the search for rocks,
Saw the land, the sky glide past.

My boat will complete the journey.
I do not know where the winding river leads.
I do not ask who will arrive.

I do not look downwards
As I reach the waterfall –
Midstream and faithful to the current.

There is no wind –
Only the power of the water.

MONTAGU DON

Writer, gardener, broadcaster, Herefordshire

M y technique for coping with depression is shaky at best and decidedly ineffective half the time, but...

The first thing I do is to get outside. It doesn't matter what weather or time of year it is, it is essential to go out of doors. Just walking is good but doing something is better. Gardening is the obvious thing, but it has to be a clearly defined simple project, like weeding a particular bed or planting out some trays of seedlings. Whatever you do must be specific and modest in ambition. The idea is to forget about yourself and concentrate on the doing.

When things are very bad, I can't do much but I do physically fight it. This last winter I spent a week concentrating on keeping my head up. Sounds silly, but it took all my energy and it worked. Holding my head up made me look out, whereas everything longed just to drop forward and look down. The world makes one sad and angry, but the only cause of depression is yourself. So all the obvious things to make you like yourself do actually help. I cut my hair, take exercise, shave, make an effort to wear nice clothes. These things can be hard and appear hopelessly superficial, but they do help.

And best of all is to have someone who loves you.

Alexa de Ferranti

London

Among things that didn't interest me (parking legally, Welsh hill fortifications, leaving my bed, Dungeons and Dragons, children), boxing had its own special status as something dull and incomprehensible and wrong. But, although I still have yet to see a live boxing match, I sometimes think that boxing saved my life. This is how and why that came about.

In the summer of 1996, I went to see *When We Were Kings*, a film about the heavyweight boxing championship between Mohammed Ali and George Foreman in Zaire. I was recommended the film by a friend who was an usher at the cinema. Incapable of saying no to anything, I arranged to meet her and bought a ticket.

I had a self-appointed role as defender of the status quo and it never failed to provide its shy satisfactions. The opposite of boxing, my title went forever unchallenged – no gloves required, no ring, no audience, no referee – the only task to ensure no one won – not me, not anyone. I demur, therefore I am. Peacemaker, Forgiver of the Misguided, Protector of the Timid, I was quietly righteous, my cheek nobly turned, invisible martyr. Demands and objections were not my field, kicking and screaming neither gratifying nor necessary.

I'd been like this for longer than I could remember. Consciousness had evolved piecemeal, with it a dim resignation, a back-handed making of room for more confident little girls, a disdain for their efforts seen spent and rewarded. Slyly I befriended self-believers, secretly patronising them, comfortable in the knowledge that no good ever came of striving. As for the people who actually pushed themselves, stared life between the eyes, ignored the disapproval of others, my contempt knew no bounds.

Behaviour like that was grotesque and no doubt caused war, famine and untold suffering.

But 30 years of suppressed rage and envy started leaking into my life. If avoidance of confrontation had been my goal, superiority, books and an ocean of sleep my rewards, I was at an utter loss to identify who or what it was I was meant to confront, and what might lie beyond. My imagination collapsed. Nothing was possible, nothingness an increasingly appealing idea. This then was my state of mind, wedged into my cinema seat on Upper Street that summer.

Sitting staring at the curtains, gently putrefying, I busied myself trying to organise my innards – stomach down, brain up, heart left – my eyes were closed when the film started. An eerie, urgent panting had become very loud, something inside me had found a way of taking in extra oxygen, a sound full of malign intent. I felt afraid and opened my eyes. The screen was full of face, a shining face with staring eyes and agile lips, a woman's face, designed to be looked at. Something had happened. My heart snapped into place, wanting to catch up with the frantic rhythm on the screen. The woman's face disappeared but the sound continued. I struggled to understand a series of quick-fire images that followed – black and white footage of French soldiers manhandling Africans, boys somersaulting down a dusty lane. Then a voice saying 'When we get to Africa, we're going to get it on 'coz we don't get along!'

Then I knew I was about to learn why millions of people love Mohammed Ali. It was the first time in six months I'd been able to absorb anything, and the 120 minutes that followed was a luxury holiday from myself. I was embraced by the story, engulfed by history, infected with desire, out of body, in love. Shot through with my favourite music soothingly punctuated by interviews with sport intellectuals, the film explained the extraordinary events leading up to the Rumble in the Jungle and it's most unlikely outcome – the triumph of Mohammed Ali. The footage of boxing matches, the parts I'd hoped to loathe, I found utterly gripping. My attention was at its peak during the fight scenes and training sessions – knockouts, holds, jabs, right hooks, the pummelling of the heavy bag. I relished each blow. The violence seemed necessary, meaningful, the whole sport a cruel, essential ritual expressing everything about the world I had chosen to ignore for 30 years. I have watched the film umpteen times since; scrutinising the fight scenes like some has-been ruminating on comeback.

I left the cinema on a high which lasted a day or so, during which time I bought every book about boxing I could lay my hands on. Then I reassumed the position – bed, screening calls, stale cereal, off milk. I read and slept and read and slept and read, thinking about my life in the context of this weird, marvellous sport. It wasn't just Ali, that walking superlative, I loved; everything about boxing held up a mirror to the world – a brutal, cruel, ugly world laced with beauty, dignity, grace, absurdity. I hadn't realised these things could thrive in such proximity, and nowhere perhaps do they more closely than in boxing.

My birthday came round – there was a party on a boat which couldn't leave its mooring due to excess wind. At a hen night, the tarot reader told me to stay at home and watch TV for the foreseeable future. I continued hovering on the seabed, a dark-zone mussel, waiting and dreaming of butterflies, bees, right hooks and skipping ropes. It was time to climb up into the ring.

JEREMY CLARKE

Journalist, South Devon

Depression is blankness. Blank nothingness. Your mind is adrift in a cold emotionless space, where there is no past, no present and no future.

You peer at the mirror, surprised that the misery you are dragging round with you has a human face; your face; a horrible, staring, ugly face; a face best not seen too much in public. Eventually you take this face and point it at a doctor. You feel a fraud because you are not ill. On the contrary, you think you are seeing the world as it really is for the first time since the last time you felt like this.

The doctor, having held a position of inordinate power for many years, won't be able to sympathise, but he may offer condolences. 'Any corresponding ups?' he'll say. Sadly no, you answer. 'Thinking of killing yourself?'

You are, you tell him. (Though your interest in your own termination is more detached and academic than he probably imagines.)

The doctor reaches for his prescribing pad, or taps at his keyboard. Much better for you if he prescribes an old-fashioned fast-acting antidepressant like Imipramine or Prothiadine. But better for him if he gives you sodding Prozac. Less chance of his being sued by righteous relatives after you've accidentally overdosed. Unfortunately Prozac takes two to four weeks to take effect. So while you are waiting for the little blue capsules to increase the level of serotonin in your brain, you can't sleep, and you're worse off than you were before.

But friend, stick with it. Two weeks, two months, two years later (it's all the same when you are stuck in nothingness), without your even realising it (so imperceptible is the transition), you will find yourself back once more on the bracing poop-deck of this ship of fools.

KATE O'SULLIVAN

London

My aunt gave me my dog Tray because she was concerned about me. The first night I made her sleep at the side of my bed on the floor. She kept jumping up and whimpering and I kept pushing her back down. I thought I was doing the right thing – dog training in a way my father would have approved of – but when I told him about it the next day he said, 'That poor dog, first night away from its mother, of course you should have taken her into the bed.' After that I did and we got on famously, and in the end Tray made all the difference to me until I had children of my own.

Then somehow this story repeated itself. George was

born and the first night in hospital he was swaddled in a cell blanket and put in a plastic box next to my bed. I was very touched by him but thought that he should stay in his polypropylene case, as otherwise he would learn bad habits.

Then suddenly I remembered Tray and, with great relief and a sort of embarrassment, took him into bed and slept with him in my arms.

LEWIS WOLPERT

Professor of Biology as Applied to Medicine at

University College, London

Depression is a mental illness that can be fatal. Suicidal thoughts are all too common among depressed patients, and when I was at my most depressed I thought of little else. Though I am a biologist, I did not know how to reliably kill myself. I did not want pain and did not know what drug I could get hold of that would finish me off. I hoarded my sleeping pills and heart pills but was not sure they would work, and did not want to end up even worse off, if that was possible. In hospital, my room on the seventh floor had a large window that could not be opened. I imagined smashing it open with a chair but I knew I would be too frightened of heights to jump. I am also too much of a physical coward and frightened of pain to leap in front of a train. I imagined that there was a button next to my bed that, if pressed, would kill me painlessly and wondered if I would really push it. When I was at my home during the day, I repeatedly imagined running across the room and crashing my head through the pane in the glass door and so cutting my throat. What stopped me? My wife became very angry and said it would have an intolerable effect on her and my children. However, she agreed to help me if in a year's time my condition was unchanged. Fortunately, I believed her and so began my slow recovery, helped by the antidepressant Seroxat and cognitive therapy.

Cognitive therapy may sometimes sound like little more than common sense, but I really needed it and it helped. As I slowly improved, I contemplated going to my first committee meeting since falling ill. What my therapist helped me envisage were the likely negative possibilities; how bad would it be, for example, if I went and then had to leave.

Would my colleagues be very critical? I decided to go. Moreover, that afternoon I cycled to work for the first time in ages since getting ill. The committee meeting went well and marked a major step in my recovery.

I may also have been assisted in the early stages by what my wife Jill called my media cure. The BBC *Today* programme phoned me one evening and asked me if I would comment on the first working out of the complete DNA sequence of a cell. I agreed, and their radio car came round the next morning at about 7.30 – the first time I had been functional that early for months. The interview went well.

Anonymous

When I was depressed I did not know wholly why I was, but I knew that part of it was to do with failing my CSE exams. Ever since I was a child I'd always known that I was different, but I could not see what it was. Then last year I was diagnosed with a form of autism, called Asperger's syndrome. This was a big relief, and it gave me hope that I could meet people with similar problems. My behaviour is now a recognised problem which affects many people.

K. E. Oakley

Dear Heather,

I am sorry to hear you are having difficulties with your partner but you must remember to try and be strong. I know Josh has married your best friend when you were going to marry him, but that's no reason to try and kill yourself. Let me tell you a story.

Once, long ago, a young girl married very young because she was in love. Her parents didn't approve but when they asked, 'Do you really know this man? Have you been going out long enough? Shouldn't you wait a year?' she answered, 'Well I've known him longer than you knew each other before you got married!' It was cruel, but the girl was far too in love to care. Cruelty and love happen.

Well, time went on and the planning began in earnest. Yes, it was a romantic white wedding. Both families joined in. Everyone had their ideas and politeness meant the bride had a large wedding when she would have preferred a small one; the groom couldn't fly, though the bride would have preferred him to treat her to some sea and sand and foreign climes, but he made her settle for Cornwall!

The wedding day dawned and when she was dressed the bride told her father, 'No I can't get married,' and she was told it was just nerves. So it went ahead and they were married. To cut a long story short, the young girl knew when she came off the honeymoon that it wasn't going to be a dream ride. In fact she wanted to get off! But this girl just got on making a happy home, cooking, cleaning, washing, ironing, etc., because the new husband did not help with anything; he worked. But so did she. He earned and smoked; she worked full time.

I'm sorry, Heather, I seem to be rambling. The point of this whole story is that she came home one night and

cooked the tea as usual. They sat, as they did, watching television and then they had an almighty row and he accused her of an affair. Well, the girl was so upset because she hadn't looked at another man and for the one person she thought she loved most on this earth to say that... the betrayal made her take *an overdose*. She went into their bedroom and lay on the bed desperate to die, thinking it was over, when a glimmer of hope sparked in her mind. Why was she killing herself? Why? He wasn't worth it.

Heather, listen, that girl realised something that you should. People aren't worth it. No person can be worth dying over. Your life is precious. Live it to the full. It is no dress rehearsal. Go for it! So I've told you about this girl, but now I'll tell you that that girl was me when I was young. Yes, your friend Jasmine. Now I am strong, proud and single and you can be too.

Love Jasmine

RICK STROUD

Film director, Chelsea, London

Here is a poem I wrote when I was very depressed and in group therapy. The world seemed very pointless then.

Greeting Card

I think of you my dearest dear

Down all the days we never went
In all the songs we never sang
In all the sounds we never heard
And all the love we never made.

Through all the peace we never gave
And all the truth we never told

In all the guilt
In all the pain
In all the silence
All the blame

I'll think of you again my dear
But not today or yesterday
Not now or then or sometime soon,
But whenever we are happy.

ALISON NADEL

Writer and journalist, London

One of my favourite stories used to be about a woman who decides to take up running. She's fat and unfit and it's slow work. But gradually, she gets faster until, ultimately, she is able to run without stopping. And she does. One evening, while her husband and children are eating pizza with the television blaring, she puts on her trainers and says good-bye. They ignore her. So she runs. She runs and runs.

This used to be the way I'd react to depression. For as long as I can remember, I've experienced spells of torturous emptiness, despite the appearance of a very full life; times of searing loneliness, despite the presence of many friends. I kept my despair a secret. I was ashamed. I was terrified that I might be going mad. Anyway, what had I to complain about? Outwardly, I had everything. But the worse I felt inside, the faster I ran, hoping to escape by perfecting my outer world.

The first time I admitted to wanting to end it all was to an elderly doctor while I was a student. Grudgingly, he gave me some pills, warned me that they might make my mouth dry, patted me on the bottom and said, 'What's a pretty girl like you got to be upset about?' Exactly. I wasn't an Ethiopian watching her baby die of starvation. I just felt a complete failure and had no hope that I would ever have hope again. Even when I took all the pills that the doctor had given me and slept for 48 hours, I woke up cursing myself that I had failed to commit suicide.

There is something devastating about the first time you realise that you want to kill yourself. I did not kill myself because a friend did. He, too, was young. He, too, seemed to have everything anyone could wish for. The impact of his death was so devastating to so many people that suicide ceased to be an option. One evening, I made a pact with my sister, who was also struggling with depression, that neither of us was allowed to do it. We realised that one death would kill both of us. That didn't mean that the wish to die went away. But each time it came back, it lost some of its charge and was no longer something to feel devastated about. Increasingly, it began to feel logical but impossible.

My outer life continued to perfect itself. I married a lovely man; we had a gorgeous baby girl, a fascinating life in Hong Kong and my career as a journalist was at its peak. Then one day, suddenly, I found it hard to walk. I was wearing my favourite old suede shoes and was rushing, late as usual, for lunch with friends at one of the city's best restaurants. I could barely move, my feet felt as heavy as blocks of concrete. I thought I'd just strained some muscles. Within two weeks, not just the ability, but also the desire to walk had gone. A few weeks after that, the journey from my bed to the shower became the biggest challenge of the day. I stopped seeing colours; light hurt my eyes. I stopped sleeping, was barely eating or talking and had to hand over the care of my baby girl to my amazing nanny.

It took months before I was given the label 'depression'. It took two years to find a doctor who was able to respond with empathy and treat the illness. Meanwhile, I tried and failed to respond to every antidepressant available. The pain of those years is indescribable. Paradoxically, I survived because I was so good at denying the pain. I was brilliant at guilt. It was my fault that I'd got into this state. I felt apologetic. I felt desperately alone. But it took too much energy to go out or maintain the false front. Being with other people was too painful – any contact was like acid on bare skin. Depression forced me to stop running. I was stuck with myself; a person who felt as significant as a single dried pea.

One of my exceptional friends refused to give up calling and, one day, bundled me out to an exhibition to be shown around by the curator. It was there that I saw a painting by a Dada artist who had ripped up a painting, thrown it onto a piece of canvas and stuck the pieces together where they fell. It made perfect sense. I knew that my life had been shredded to pieces but I was to learn that this was one of the greatest gifts – the chance to rebuilt it completely.

The agony of depression forced me into therapy and the eviscerating process of revisiting the horror of my childhood and unlearning all the ways I had learned to cope. My therapist was remarkable. I felt so sorry for her having to sit with a client who was as responsive as an Egyptian mummy. But she refused to give up. One of the greatest things that she did for me was to allow me to be depressed.

Then, with the help of a new psychiatrist's ingenious cocktail of antidepressants, I began to sleep again. I began to get glimpses of life without the crushing weight of despair. The first was a drop of water on the wall of the shower. It was like a jewel radiating colour. It was perfect. I could see it. I burst into his office ranting about the drop of water and the fact that I was beginning to have hope again. I thanked him profusely believing that the pills were fixing me. His response was shocking. He said that if I was to have any chance of recovery I had to rewire the whole of my thinking. This is the man I now credit with saving my

life, but, at that point, if I'd had an AK47, I would have used it.

I read everything I could from the cheesiest self-help books to obscure theories from ancient philosophies. I tried every alternative therapy available. But these were other people's solutions, not my own. The only way for me was to find my own way, and this meant dropping all the analysis and judgment and learning one of the hardest things of all – to stop running and to allow myself to feel.

The process of recovery was not a matter of weeks but years. Most of this time was spent behind a thick Perspex screen. I could observe situations that I knew should make me happy but I could not feel anything but pain. My daughter's first steps, her delight at the candles on her birthday cake, my loving husband's tender attempts to help – all of this felt like nothing. But, agonisingly slowly, the moments of freedom from depression became hours, then whole days, and then weeks. The dried pea didn't grow into a rose garden but a tangled thicket of raw emotion – anger, fear, hate, love, gratitude and faith.

Five years on, I now live in London and still take anti-depressants and have just gone back into therapy. But I am happier now than I've ever known it possible to be. The opposite of depression is not joy but vitality. To be alive feels like a miracle. Without depression, there is nothing normal about normal life, it's fantastic. Depression is no longer an abyss that I could randomly trip back into. It comes and goes like a rare storm. I now take it as a call to wake up, not to sleep. What is it I am not feeling? What is it that I am trying to run from?

BRENDA FRICKER

Actress

Life has little direction without hope. Kindness can touch it, I think. Intelligence too. And humour smashes down the big, black door that locks hope out.

HUGH ST CLAIR

Interior design consultant, Norfolk

It's not who or what I love but what I hate that lifts me from the cloying miasma of despondency that engulfs me from time to time. I can get no pleasure out of beautiful things when I am depressed. Sunlight streams through the window on to a beautiful emerald green and gold bedspread, (I remember clearly the thrill of finding it in a junk shop), and bounces off the blue glass lamps that in high times I find so beautiful. However, when I am feeling low, they fail to lift my spirits and I stare vacantly beyond them. Nothing stimulates me more than beautiful objects, except when I am depressed and then I notice nothing. When I am feeling good I find ideas of sport, competition and team spirit pointless. I prefer individual pursuits, where I can be in control. Yet when I am in a deep gloom, the only way to blow the blues away is by taking physical exercise. It requires a gargantuan effort for me to get up and do it, but having made that effort to participate in a sport, I feel an extraordinary sense of achievement. I can't say I enjoy it because I am the worst possible sportsman, almost to the point of being disabled. I have no hand-to-eye co-ordination and seldom win a game, but for me that is immaterial. It's more a question of survival against almost always superior opponents, which distracts me from my own thoughts and a world which I normally inhabit.

JULIA

Primary School Teacher, Maidenhead

'But I being poor, have only my dreams;
I have spread my dreams under your feet;
Tread softly, because you tread on my dreams.'

W.B. Yeats

Someone not only trod on my dreams, he trampled upon them; and then, when I had picked them up, renewed them, and laid them elsewhere, he sought them out again and stamped on them. Uncaring and pitiless. He was the kindest person I knew, and now has been more cruel than the sum of all previous detractors. How then to recover hope?

The pastoral care of my priest. He was witty, wise and kind. He always managed to make me laugh.

The professional care of my counsellor. He did everything right.

The concerned care of neighbours, acquaintances, work-mates. A touch, a smile, a wave, a word – all showed support and understanding.

The loving care of friends. Some showed total commitment, and were quite unafraid about the extent to which they became involved.

Practical support – lifts, shopping, information, gardening, meals.

Financial support – cheques for taxis, food, solicitors, even a dental bill!

Emotional support – people came, people invited me to their homes, to their functions. People took me out and people phoned. One friend still phones every Sunday.

Then there was the neutral benefit afforded by the books I read. Reading fiction, notably *Girl with a Pearl Earring*, by Tracey Chevalier, and *Enduring Love*, by Ian McEwan.

I looked outside myself, enabling different, albeit vicarious experiences.

Reading *Self-esteem* by Gael Lindenfeld and *The Road less Travelled* by M. Scott Peck, I looked inside myself, enabling gentle, non-partisan introspection.

Finally – my son and my daughter – their existence.

JOSEPH MCWILLIAMS

Painter and President of the Royal Ulster

Academy of Arts Belfast

A spark of intensity

'Stand with both your feet together. Stand up straight; that's right. Now keep your arms by your side. Good boy. Now close your eyes.'

I held my eyes tightly closed and felt a slight wobbling sensation.

'How often does he have these... ahem, dizzy spells?'

'He says he gets them coming home from school, Doctor, but I'm sure that it was only after that boy hit him on the head with a piece of wood.' My mother had convinced herself, and it seemed the doctor, that a classroom incident involving the lid of a wooden desk was responsible for my occasional 'dizzy spells'.

I can't remember the ensuing conversation btween my mother and the medic, but it ended with him saying to me as he wrote a prescription, 'Take one of these tablets in the morning and one at night.'

It was 1954. I was 15 years of age and I had just been given a prescription for barbiturates for no good reason.

*

One night in 1962, I left a student party. The bonhomie and merriment of my friends had failed to extricate me from the deepening gloom in my head. It was late at night. The bus service had stopped. I decided to walk the three-mile journey home across Belfast's dingy, deserted streets. My echoing footsteps accompanied me like a stranger's. Then, suddenly, in an instant, my perception altered. The once familiar streets had become an alien landscape. Just as a familiar word, when scrutinised, becomes a strange configuration on the page, the street had been transformed into an eerie, empty stage set. I was filled with an over-whelming dread. What little control I had over my anxiety disappeared in a crescendo of panic. I began to run. The irrationality of the action made my terror even more acute. My heart pounded as I stumbled fitfully along the streets, clinging close to the walls of the houses for some imagined protection. I ran, walked, stumbled and staggered until at last I approached my home. I felt as though I had left a battlefield. The intensity of the panic began to subside; but I had passed a personal Rubicon and life would never be the same again. For a brief period that night, I had lost control of my most cherished attribute – my mind – and the future looked as dark as madness.

*

I sought psychiatric help at one of the newly created day clinics. The psychiatrist I met was authoritative without being patronising, an unusual feature in a doctor at that time. He expressed amazement that I had been prescribed for eight years increasing doses of Phenobarbitone without any reappraisals of my complaint.

'The first thing we'll have to do,' he said, 'is to rule out any possible problems in the central nervous system, such as epilepsy'. A series of hospital tests did this.

'...The second thing we have to do, is to get you off barbiturates. It won't be easy. You will have to kick the habit.'

I hadn't been aware that I had a habit to kick. I was still depressed, still anxious, and agoraphobic; 23 years of age and I had to be accompanied by my mother on the morning's one-mile walk to the clinic. But I was faintly glad that I was getting off this drug and faintly hopeful that something was being done.

I placed all my hope on the sessions with the psychiatrist. But still I didn't notice any significant improvement in my mental state. My anxiety lost some of its potency, but this was only because depression took over. I was filled with a growing terror that it might never go away. My nights were plagued with anxiety-driven dreams and mornings would burst upon me with a ferocious hopelessness.

Then something marvellously unexpected happened: a change in the pattern. One night during my customary unquiet sleep, a dream occurred, almost subliminal in its brevity. I was kissing a girl and I was in love with her. Then the dream ended, fleeting as a frame of a film. The next morning, I awakened to face the usual joyless day. Nothing had changed. The world was still drained of its colour.

As I made my way to the clinic, I recalled the dream. Initially I wondered why a girl whom I barely knew had figured in it. Then with a shock I realized that in that brief, subconscious encounter I had been happy. This mind which seemed incapable of joy had generated in my dream a little spark of intensity, a fragment of hope. I clutched at the thought – if I can experience such happiness in a dream, then my mind must still be functioning in that mode. Somewhere submerged within my consciousness lies this wonderful normality waiting to be salvaged. I had no idea how this could be achieved, but as I reached the clinic that morning I felt a tingle in my thinking as though in some deep recess something dormant was awakening.

Some days later I told the psychiatrist that I intended

leaving the clinic to complete my final year at college.

'Good. You must feel a lot better?'

'Not really, but I can't stay here all my life.'

He wished me well, and I left. I remember feeling a real sense of determination as I walked out of the building, because I knew that I wasn't accepting a cure, I was simply accepting myself.

Easter was approaching and lines from **T.S. Eliot's** 'Ash Wednesday' came into my head:

'Teach us to care and not to care
Teach us to sit still.'

In the weeks which followed, no miraculous transformation took place. A monotony of grey days still stretched ahead; but, like my dream, little patches of light began to filter through.

At first they would steal upon me unawares; then, almost imperceptibly, their frequency increased until I was conscious that a whole somnolent world of the senses was reawakening. The spring of that year held all the hope that springtime should and the future began to look like a like-able place.

And the girl in my dreams? Well, maybe there was a touch of the miraculous. We met, fell in love and got married. But that was 35 years ago, and my son and daughter have just read this little account for the first time.

CAROLINE MOOREHEAD

Journalist and writer

When Primo Levi started falling into the depressions that clouded the last year of his life, he would ask his friends: 'Am I going to be all right?' This haunting question, all too familiar to those who spend time in depression's grey land, tormented Levi's friends, as it torments all those who hear it. During two long bad spells of depression, I asked it constantly myself. At the time it seemed to me to be a question of faith, of belief, not only that I would in fact get better, but that I was of sufficient worth for it to matter whether I got better or not. Later, I came to see it as about the nature of friendship.

It is a fact that no one who has not been profoundly

depressed is able to comprehend its horror and its loneliness; they can listen, sympathise and imagine, but they cannot feel. Primo Levi used to say that what he experienced in Auschwitz was not as bad as what he went through when in the grip of what he chose simply to call 'being down'. But just as Levi learnt about humanity – what it was to be a man – in the camps, I learnt about friendship in the course of being depressed.

Like Levi, I was fortunate enough to have remarkable friends. There were people in my life who had never themselves been deeply depressed but who found some capacity within themselves to convince me that this miasma of dread would pass; that they knew beyond all doubt that it would and they would stick with me until it did. And in the process they gave me a feeling that I mattered and, perhaps more importantly, that they needed me. Not just as a companion, but as an integral part of their landscapes, and that without me, those landscapes would be a permanently poorer place. The assumption, which did not seem to need to be stated, was that depression, like extreme loss or grief, was just another hideous endurance test in Stevie Smith's enemy territory. We had shared other terrible things; we would, naturally, share this. And so, like Leonardo, the Italian worker who, by giving Levi extra bread demonstrated that humanity was something worth surviving for, they taught me the nature of friendship, the almost tangible sustaining power of genuine affection; something that went well beyond the need to understand precisely what I was going through. I was not alone.

VICKI FEAVER

Poet

Pills

For God's sake take your pills!
He had to hurl her against the bathroom wall
before she'd be silent.
He wanted peace in the house.
He wanted her tame, grateful, faithful,
to eat from his hand
the little yellow pills
that turned everything grey
as a sea fret: butter strings of marmalade,
crumbs crusted round the children's mouths
like grey sand. Take three tablets
three times a day. She'd push them up
with her tongue between teeth and cheek,
spitting them into the sink. After a few days,
when the mist rolled back, she'd strain her neck

craning to comprehend the blue space
birds moved in, limitless, filled
with twitterings and cries.
She'd kneel on the lawn,
skirt soaked, rediscovering
the shades of grass: each blade –
like the seconds lost –
separate, sharp, drawing blood
from her thumb. She'd gaze at oranges
as people gaze at statues of Christ
on the Cross: the brilliant rinds –
packed with juice, flesh, pips –
exploding like grenades,
like brains, like trapped gases
at the surface of the sun.

JAMES FORREST

London

If you can concentrate on reading this book, then there is hope yet. And if you can cope with hope, you can deal with despair.

WILLIAM FIENNES

Author

I waited for my condition to improve. I wasn't patient. The edge of my fear rubbed off as the weeks passed, but I became depressed. In hospital, I had longed to return to the environment I knew better than any other, because it was something of which I could be sure; because the familiar – the *known* – promised sanctuary from all that was confusing, alien and new. But after a while the complexion of the familiar began to change. The house, and the past it contained, seemed more prison than sanctuary. As I saw it, my friends were proceeding with their lives, their appetites and energies undimmed, while I was being held back against my will, penalized for an offence of which I was entirely ignorant. My initial relief that the crisis had passed turned slowly to anger, and my frustrations were mollified but not resolved by the kindness of those close to me, because no one, however loving, could give me the one thing I wanted above all else: my former self...

...My mother suggested a change of scene, and we drove to a hotel close to the Welsh border. We had no idea it would be the venue for a ladies' professional golf tournament. Each morning, before breakfast, I walked down to the practice tees to watch the women loosen up their swings. I found *The Snow Goose* and read it straight through, remembering Mr. Faulkner, the room's high windows, the grooved desks. I was suspicious of the story's sentimentality, its glaze of religious allegory, the easy portentousness of its abstract nouns, and I laughed at Gallico's attempts to render phonetically (as if they were birdsong) the East End speech of the soldiers in the pub and the upper-class diction of the officers. But something in the story haunted me...

...When we came back from the hotel, I wanted to learn about birds. I couldn't shake *The Snow Goose* from my head. I wandered round the garden, equipped with my father's Zeiss pocket binoculars and a simple beginner's field guide, looking for birds, trying to learn their names. Sometimes I'd describe a bird to my father and he'd name it for me: goldfinch, blackcap, yellowhammer. It must have been a surprise for my parents to see me showing these signs of enthusiasm: for months I'd been sullen, despondent, introverted, caught up in my own fears, resentful that my life had been interrupted so violently. In hospital, I'd longed to be at home. But by the end of May I was sick of it – restless, hungry for new experiences, different horizons. When I read Gallico's descriptions of the flights of geese, I wondered at the mysterious signals that told a bird it was time to move, time to fly.

I shared it, this urge to go. I was getting stronger. I was strong enough to be curious. It was as if I were trying to redeem my earlier failure to notice, the way I gave my attention, as I never had done as a child, to the swallows, swifts, rooks, wagtails, finches, warblers, thrushes and woodpeckers around the house – my father ready with a name, a habit, a piece of lore. I loved the swifts most of all. I'd never watched them so intently. My father said that after they left the house at the beginning of August many of them wouldn't land or touch down until they came back to nest the following May: they drank on the wing, fed on the wing, even slept on the wing. I thought of Gallico's snow goose flying south from the Arctic each autumn, the pink-footed and barnacle geese moving back and forth between Rhayader's sanctuary and their northern breeding grounds. Why did birds undertake such journeys? How did they know when to go, or where? How did swifts, year after year, find their way from Malawi to this house, my child-hood home?

I was excited about something for the first time since I'd fallen ill, and I needed a project, a distraction, a means of escape. I carried books about bird migration up to a room at the top of the house, a real cubby-hole, tucked in under the roof, its low ceiling mottled with sooty drifts and rings, as if candles had smoked runes on to the cracked plaster – a room we knew as the eyrie, because it had the high, snug feeling of an eagle's nest. The pattern of fields I could see through the little two-light window was second nature to me, and I knew what each field was called: Lower Quarters, Danvers Meadow, Morby's Close, Allowance Ground. Sometimes swifts screamed past the window as I sat in the eyrie, studying ornithology.

(*William Fiennes wrote* The Snow Geese *after recovering from a serious illness.*)

GERARD MANLEY HOPKINS

My own heart let me more have pity on; let
Me live to my sad self hereafter kind,
Charitable; not live this tormented mind
With this tormented mind tormenting yet.

I cast for comfort I can no more get
By groping round my comfortless, than blind
Eyes in their dark can day or thirst can find
Thirst's all-in-all in all a world of wet.

Soul, self; come, poor Jackself, I do advise
You, jaded, let be; call off thoughts awhile
Elsewhere; leave comfort root-room; let joy size

At God knows when to God knows what; whose smile
's not wrung; see you; unforeseen times rather – as
skies
Betweenpie mountains – lights a lovely mile.

POSTCRIPT

When it first happened I vowed I would never take pills, I would get better by myself, and make sure it never happened again. After that, I had a further four relapses in five years. I overcame my fear of pills and was helped enormously by them as well as by therapy. But I could never say never again, not even now when I have a love I never could have dreamt might happen to me. I am doing my best to avoid it, but up to a point I can only hope.

When I first met my psychiatrist she said something which seemed profoundly inappropriate at the time – that one day I would be able to see my depression as a gift. Only now am I able to look back at the person I was ten years ago and see someone who was bravely trying to carry several worlds on her shoulders. 'This isn't your fault' were the words a therapist said to me after my first breakdown. They started a slow and painful process of unravelment, a shedding of the armour that I thought was me, something I wouldn't and couldn't have done without hitting the bottom and having to do it. I've come to terms with my vulnerability and I'm grateful for it. I can receive and give love in a way I didn't know how to. I agree with Kay Redfield Jamison, who says in her book *The Unquiet Mind*, that of all things love is the most healing.

...I understand the word love in the broadest sense, and not exclusively to mean the true love of a soul mate.

Flora McDonnell

Copyright ©

The Ted Hughes Estate. 'A Bedtime Story' was taken from the collection *The Crow*.

Anna Kamienska. Poem taken from '*Two Darknesses: Selected Poems* (Flambard, 1994). Translated from the Polish by Tomasz Krzeszowski and Desmond Graham.

William Wordsworth. Verse taken from Book VI, 'Cambridge and the Alps', *The Prelude*, 1805 version.

Andrew Solomon. Extract printed with the permission of the author from *The Noonday Demon: An Atlas of Depression* (Simon & Schuster, 2001).

Sidney Smith. Letter to Lady Georgiana Morpeth, taken from *The Letters of Sidney Smith*.

Alice Oswald. Poem taken from *The Thing in the Gap-Stone Stile*, first published in Oxford Poets as an OUP paperback in 1996.

John Montague. Poem printed with the permission of the author.

Charlotte Raven Extract from article published concurrently in the *Observer* and the *New Statesman*, 17.3.02

Kay Redfield Jamison Extract printed with the permission of the author from *An Unquiet Mind* (Alfred A Knopf, 1995).

Wendy Cope. Poem reproduced with the author's permission.

Lewis Wolpert. Extract printed with the permission of the author from *Malignant Sadness* (Faber & Faber, 2001)

W.B. Yeats. Lines from 'He Wishes for the Cloths of Heaven', by W.B. Yeats, printed with the permission of A.P. Watt Ltd., on behalf of Michael B. Yeats)

T.S.Eliot. Lines from 'Ash Wednesday' from *The Complete Poems* of T. S. Eliot, published by Faber & Faber.

Vicky Feaver. This poem first appeared in *Mind Readings: Writers' Journeys Through Mental States* (Minerva, 1996).

William Fiennes. Printed with the permission of the author, from *The Snow Geese* (Picador, 2002)

Acknowledgements

I would like to thank Dr. Brenda Davies for her help and support during the concept of this book. I would also like to thank Felicity Rubenstein for her advice; Virginia Ironside, for her help and encouragement; and Marie Heaney; Aisling Foster; Raffaella St. Clair; Emma Craigy; Jock Encombe; John Julius Norwich; Laura Cecil; local Mind offices and the charity Mind Out for Mental Health, as well any other people I may have forgotten, for putting me in touch with several of the people who have written for this book.

Above all, I would like to thank everyone who has contributed to this book for their courage and generosity.

Useful Addresses

AWARE

72 Lower Leeson Street, Dublin 2, Republic of Ireland

Tel: (01) 6766166 (Every day, 10am–10pm)

Provides information and support to people affected by depression in Ireland and Northern Ireland

THE ASSOCIATION OF POST-NATAL ILLNESS

25 Jerdan Place, Fulham, London SW6 1BE

Tel: 020 7386 0868

Information from people who have had similar experiences

THE BRITISH ASSOCIATION FOR COUNSELLING

1 Regent Place, Rugby, Warwickshire, CV21 2PJ

Tel: 01788 550 899 (8.45am–4.45pm)

Provides information and advice on all matters related to

counselling. They can also send you a list of accredited coun-
sellors in your local area

THE BRITISH ASSOCIATION FOR BEHAVIOURAL AND COGNITIVE PSYCHOTHERAPIES

PO Box 9, Accrington, BB5 2GD. Tel/fax: 01254 875277
Can provide a directory of registered therapists

CALM

0800 585858 (Everyday, 5pm–3am)
Helpline for young men who are depressed or suicidal

CARERS LINE

0808 808 7777 (Mon-Fri 10.00-12.00, 14.00-1600)
Helpline providing advice for carers on any issue

CRUSE

Bereavement Care, Cruse House, 126 Sheen Road,
Richmond, Surrey, TW9 1UR. Tel: 020 8940 4818
(helpline & information line Mon–Fri, 9.30–5pm)
Information and advice for people who are bereaved

HEALTH INFORMATION SERVICE

0800 665 544 (Mon–Fri, 9.00–17.00 (may vary according to locality)

Information on all health-related subjects including where to get treatment

LESBIAN AND GAY BEREAVEMENT PROJECT

Unitarian Rooms, Hoop Lane, London, NW11 ORL

Tel: 020 7403 5969

Offers support and counselling for bereavement and AIDS

THE MANIC DEPRESSION FELLOWSHIP

Castle Works, 21 St. Georges Road, London, SE1 6ES.

National Advice Line: 020 7793 2600; Scotland Advice Line: 0141 560 2050; Wales Advice Line: 01633 244 244 (Mon–Thurs 9am–4pm, Fri 9am–5pm)

Produces information and advice specifically related to Manic Depression or bipolar disorder

MEDICATION AND DRUGS HELPLINE

020 7919 2999 (Mon–Fri, 11–17.00)

*Confidential information about prescription drugs
from trained medical professionals*

MIND (NATIONAL ASSOCIATION FOR MENTAL
HEALTH)
Granta House, 15-19 Broadway, London, E15 4BQ
Tel: 08457 660 163 (Mon–Fri, 9.15am–16.45pm)
Information service for matters relating to mental health

NATIONAL PHOBICS SOCIETY
0870 7700456 (Mon–Fri, 10.30–16.00)
www.phobics-society.org.uk
*Helpline for people affected by anxiety, phobias, compulsive
disorders, or panic attacks*

PACE
020 7697 0017 (Mon–Thurs, 10.00–21.00)
*Counselling, mental health advocacy and group work
for lesbians and gay men*

PARENTLINE

080 800 2222 (Mon–Fri 9.00–21.00)
Helpline and information for parents in distress

RELATE NATIONAL OFFICE
Herbert Gray College, Little Church Street, Rugby, CV21
3AP. Tel: 01788 573 241
Offers counselling on relationship problems for couples or indi-
viduals

ROYAL COLLEGE OF PSYCHIATRISTS
17 Belgrave Square, London, SW1X 8PG
Tel: 020 7235 2351
Offers information about mental illness

S.A.D ASSOCIATION
PO BOX 989 , Steyning, West Sussex, BN44 3HG
Provides information and advice on season affective disorder

THE SAMARITANS
46 Marshall Street, London, W1V 1LR
Tel: 08457 90 90 90 (24 hours, every day)

Offer confidential emotional support to any person who is suicidal or despairing

SANELINE
08457 67 80 00 (Every day 14.00–00.00)

SCOTTISH ASSOCIATION FOR MENTAL HEALTH
Cumbria House, 15 Carlton Court, Glasgow, G5 9JP
Tel: 0141 568 7000
Support, information and advice on various aspects of mental health

YOUNG MINDS PARENTS INFORMATION LINE
0800 0182138 (Mon & Fri 10–1pm, Tues, Wed & Thurs 9–4pm)
Helpline offering information and support on young peoples' mental health for parents

DEPRESSION ALLIANCE CONTACT DETAILS
National Office
Depression Alliance, 35 Westminster Bridge Road,

London, SE1 7JB. Tel: 0207 633 0557; Fax: 0207 633 0559

Scotland
Depression Alliance Scotland, 3 Grosvenor Gardens,
Edinburgh EH12 5JU. Tel: 0131 467 3050

Cymru (Wales)
Depression Alliance Cymru (Wales), 11 Plas Melin,
Westbourne Road, Whitchurch,Cardiff CF4 2BT. Tel:
02920 692 891

Flora McDonnell is an award-winning writer and illustrator of children's books. She lives in London and Ireland.